Home Protectors: A Guide to Safeguarding Your Property Against Squatters

Home Protectors: A Guide to Safeguarding Your Property Against Squatters

Copyright © 2024 by **Alheri Farouq**

TABLE OF CONTENT

Introduction

One day, you arrive home to discover strangers inhabiting your house. They assert their entitlement to the premises and persist in their refusal to depart. This inconceivable scenario epitomizes the dreaded nightmare of squatting — a situation wherein people illicitly take up residence in a property without any legal ownership or right thereof. As a homeowner, you may find the invasion of your property by squatters deeply violating and distressing.

Squatting: an action that transcends mere inconvenience or legal technicality--it directly challenges the fundamental concept of a home. Our homes embody more than just four walls; they symbolize our paramount financial investment, serve as locales where we construct lives and forge indelible memories with cherished ones. They function as sanctuaries: refuge points from an often tumultuous world. Strangers stripping away that sense of security and ownership can inflict profound emotional trauma.

Regrettably, many underestimate the prevalence of squatting: a disconcerting reality that property owners across our nation confront daily. The prime targets often include vacant homes or rental properties in transitional periods between tenants. If the residents of an occupied home extend their absence, vulnerability may still persist. Squatters, upon gaining entry and establishing residence in such cases – removing them through proper legal channels can escalate into a dauntingly costly battle.

A squatting incident's financial toll reaches much further than the mere legal fees required for navigating a complex eviction process. Frequent realities include property damage, theft of belongings and post-event cleanup costs. Unsanitary living conditions like mold and sewage issues can pose health hazards that necessitate extensive remediation work. After a squatting situation, homes in worst-case scenarios may indeed become temporarily or permanently uninhabitable.

Emotionally, the impacts penetrate just as deeply: Homeowners articulate a profound sense of violation; they describe feeling not only anxious - but even unsafe – upon reentering their own property after it has been occupied by squatters. Overcoming the tremendous difficulty in acknowledging that one's home–their place of sanctuary–has been defiled is an arduous task indeed. To regain peace of mind and reestablish a sense of security, one may require an extensive period: this process often necessitates therapeutic support.

Because these consequences are far-reaching, property owners must proactively prevent squatting; allowing unlawful residency--even briefly- opens a potential legal quagmire. Such an issue could require months or years for resolution through proper channels. The persistence of a squatting situation compounds financial damages and emotional distress more as time lengthens.

Delve into this comprehensive guide, which illuminates the protection of your property rights and fortifying your home against potential squatting threats. It offers a profound exploration of squatters' rights, the legal constructs concerning property ownership along with essential preventive actions every homeowner ought to consider. Moreover, it will meticulously outline step-by-step strategies: monitoring your property; establishing proof of residency--and safeguarding it from unauthorised entry. This comprehensive guide offers an in-depth exploration of how to safeguard your property rights and defend against home invasion by squatters: a step-by-step strategy for homeowners is outlined within these pages. The focus spans from understanding the intricate nuances surrounding squatter's rights, delving into legal frameworks associated with property ownership – all while emphasizing preventative measures every homeowner should adopt. Specifically detailed are strategies encompassing regular property monitoring; establishing indisputable proof-of-residency–both crucial aspects in deterring unauthorized entries on one's premises!

This book serves as a roadmap for property owners who, unfortunately, contend with squatters. It offers comprehensive guidance on crucial aspects such as evidence gathering, eviction procedures understanding; collaboration with law enforcement entities and legal representation hiring among others. The intention is to ensure that no homeowner feels either helpless or uncertain when their residence becomes the dwelling place of unauthorized occupants.

As a property owner, you hold the fundamental rights to preserve your home's safety, security and sanctity. This guide equips you with vital knowledge: use it to take proactive steps—mitigating risks and promptly addressing any potential squatting situations. Consider your home as an impregnable castle; fortify it against those who might attempt its unlawful seizure from you. Equipped with the appropriate tools and mindset, you can actively secure your property rights while ensuring tranquility.

Part I: Understanding Squatters' Rights and Legal Framework

Before we dive into the practical strategies for preventing and addressing squatting situations, it's crucial that we establish a solid understanding of the legal landscape surrounding this complex issue. The concept of squatters' rights and the various laws governing property ownership and occupation can seem daunting at first glance. However, arming yourself with this foundational knowledge is an essential first step in effectively protecting your home.

On the surface, the idea of someone being able to inhabit a property they don't own or rent may seem baffling - even outrageous. How could the legal system possibly afford rights to trespassers and squatters? The answer lies in the centuries-old legal principles of adverse possession and the establishment of property claims through continuous occupation over an extended period of time.

Adverse possession laws, which exist in some form in most jurisdictions across the United States, were originally conceived as a means of ensuring that land didn't sit idle and unproductive indefinitely. If the legal owner abandoned or showed little interest in maintaining a property over many years, the laws allowed for a mechanism by which continuous inhabitants could potentially claim ownership after meeting strict criteria over a very long period of residence.

In modern times, however, squatters have attempted to exploit adverse possession statutes as a means of taking over properties they have no legitimate claim to - often occupied homes or those temporarily vacant. This has understandably caused great distress for lawful property owners who one day find their homes invaded and their fundamental rights of ownership called into question.

It's important to emphasize that true cases of adverse possession leading to a legitimate change of property ownership are exceedingly rare. The requirements are incredibly stringent, including being an exclusive, continuous, hostile, open and notorious occupant of the property for a period dictated by state laws - often 10-30 years in most places. Simply moving into a vacant home does not immediately grant the squatter any legal foothold.

Nevertheless, squatters sometimes use the mere existence of adverse possession laws as justification for their actions, claiming they are simply following a process to eventually gain ownership. More often, they rely on obfuscating the legal nuances to overwhelm property owners and law enforcement with complexities in hopes of being able to maintain unlawful occupation.

As property owners, the key takeaway is this: a far-reaching comprehension of property rights, legal definitions related to ownership claims and occupation, and the judicial processes for resolving squatting disputes is absolutely vital. Being well-versed in the roles and limitations of law enforcement in handling civil property matters is also critical.

Over the next two chapters, we'll undertake an in-depth examination of adverse possession and squatters' rights within the context of property laws in your jurisdiction. Understanding the legal terminology around squatting, trespassing, and unlawful occupation is important groundwork. We'll explore the established rights and protections afforded to lawful property owners as well.

With this legal foundation firmly established, we can then progress into the heart of the book - the practical prevention methods, monitoring protocols, evidence documentation practices and resources for resolving squatting incidents through official channels. Knowledge is a homeowner's greatest asset in the fight to protect their property rights against the unlawful claims of squatters.

Chapter 1: Squatters' Rights and Legal Definitions

To effectively safeguard your property rights as a homeowner, it's essential to first develop a comprehensive understanding of the legal principles that squatters may attempt to leverage in their efforts to establish residency. At the core of this issue lies the antiquated – yet still relevant in many jurisdictions – concept known as "adverse possession."

The Origins of Adverse Possession

Adverse possession is a legal doctrine with origins dating back to early English common law of the 17th century. Its original intent was to provide a framework for someone to legally claim ownership of a property if they had openly occupied and maintained the land for an extended period of time while the rightful owner failed to make any effort to reclaim possession.

In an era when land was a critical asset for agricultural productivity, adverse possession laws aimed to discourage land from sitting idle and unproductive if the owners had seemingly abandoned their claim to the property. The underlying principle was one of making efficient use of land resources.

To successfully claim adverse possession under the strict historical standards, the occupation had to meet several key criteria over a very long period of residency, often 20-30 years:

1) **Exclusive Possession** - The occupant was the sole resident, not sharing possession.

2) **Open & Notorious** - Their residency was visible and out in the open, not hidden or clandestine.

3) **Actual Possession** - They treated the property as their own residence, making improvements, paying taxes, etc.

4) **Hostile Possession** - Their possession was against the rights of the true owner and without permission.

5) **Continuous Possession** - The occupation was unbroken over the full statutory time period required by local laws.

While the specifics vary across jurisdictions, the general premise remains that adverse possession requires *longstanding, visible occupation while "hostilely" possessing the property against the owner's rights and treating it as one's own over many years.*

It's important to note that very few, if any, modern squatting cases legitimately meet the stringent criteria for adverse possession. Most are simply unlawful trespassing situations - but squatters often try to obfuscate the legal complexities to remain as long as possible.

Defining Squatters' Rights

So what exactly are "squatters' rights" then? The term itself is somewhat misleading, as squatters do not inherently possess many substantive rights at the outset of an unlawful occupation. More accurately, squatters seek to establish a basis for adverse possession claims or other legal defenses through their actions.

In simplest terms, a squatter is someone who takes up residence on a property they have no legal ownership claim or rental rights to. Often they move into vacant homes or buildings, though occupied properties can be targets as well if the owners are away.

The mere act of being present on the property as a squatter does not automatically grant them any immediate rights to remain. However, by establishing a pattern of continuous residency, squatters can attempt to make future eviction efforts more complex for property owners.

In some jurisdictions, if squatters can demonstrate they were openly residing on a property for a certain period of time (often around 30 days in many places, but this varies), the property owner must then go through formal eviction procedures. Essentially, squatters try to obfuscate their unlawful trespassing as the start of an adverse possession claim.

It's important to reiterate, though, that simply being a squatter does not mean they have any legitimate rights to the property itself. Their mere presence does not void the legal ownership rights of the property holder. But allowing a pattern of residency to become established can potentially complicate the removal process drastically.

Defining Unlawful Occupation and Trespassing

To fully understand squatters' rights – or more accurately, their lack of rights – we need to clearly define the terms around unlawfully occupying a property:

Trespassing is the illegal entry onto private property, whether a home, building, land, or any premises owned by someone else. Simply setting foot onto the premises without permission constitutes trespassing. It is a civil offense that could also rise to the level of a criminal violation if there is evident intent to commit a crime on the property.

Squatting is a form of trespassing that involves the illegal occupation and residence within a property without the owner's consent. By moving belongings in and establishing a pattern of consistent living on the premises, squatters escalate trespassing to unlawful occupation and possession of the property.

It's important to understand that trespassing and squatting, in and of themselves, do not equate to the adverse possession process used to legally claim ownership rights. They are civil offenses of unlawfully occupying property – not a legally sanctioned pathway to pursue ownership claims.

The crucial distinction is that true adverse possession cases are exceedingly rare. They require meeting numerous stringent criteria over an extended continuous period of 20-30 years in most jurisdictions. Simply being present on a property for a few weeks or months does not constitute the foundational elements of an adverse possession claim.

That said, squatters often try to muddy the legal waters by citing adverse possession principles in an attempt to obfuscate their clear trespassing violation. They may make false claims about their "rights" as occupants based on partial understandings or intentional misrepresentations of adverse possession statutes.

As a homeowner, it's vital that you understand the basic legal definitions and principles at play so you do not become misled by squatters invoking complex legal concepts out of context. Their presence on your property is unambiguously unlawful trespassing – not the start of any adverse possession process.

Jurisdictional Variances in Laws

While the core legal principles around property ownership, trespassing, squatters' rights and adverse possession have common threads, it's important to note that the specific regulations and procedures can vary significantly across different states and municipalities.

Adverse possession statutes in particular tend to differ in their details. Most jurisdictions require continuous occupation over 20-30 years to make a legitimate claim, but some states have shorter or longer time periods codified into their laws.

The criteria that must be met to demonstrate exclusive, open, hostile and continuous possession can also have nuanced differences across locales in terms of what evidence is deemed acceptable. Standards for proving payment of taxes, making improvements to the property and other benchmarks of "actual possession" vary.

Similarly, the processes for handling unlawful squatting situations are not uniform across the nation. Some states afford property owners more immediate civil remedies for quickly removing trespassers. Other jurisdictions have more stringent protocols that must be followed, potentially requiring formal eviction proceedings even for very recent squatting situations.

Certain municipalities have enacted specific local ordinances aimed at cracking down on squatting by accelerating processes for removal and imposing stiffer penalties. Conversely, some major cities have struggled with ineffective enforcement capabilities.

It cannot be overstated how critical it is to thoroughly research and understand the precise adverse possession laws, definitions of squatters' rights, legal remedies, and enforcement protocols within your specific city and state. This local knowledge forms the foundation for all strategies to prevent squatting and navigate any unlawful occupation incidents effectively.

While the fundamental principles we've discussed so far apply nearly universally, the nuanced local interpretations and processes can vary immensely. As a homeowner, you need to operate from a basis of knowing the specifics that your particular property is subject to.

In the next chapter, we'll take a deeper look at the affirmative property rights possessed by lawful owners – and the evidence necessary to demonstrate clear ownership claims. When combined with a mastery of the squatting laws specific to your locale, you'll be well-equipped to definitively assert your rightful legal standing.

From that position of understanding, we can then progress into exploring the preventative measures and evidence gathering necessary to deter squatters from ever gaining a foothold on your property in the first place. The sustained hard work of protecting your home begins with immersing yourself in the legal landscape unique to your area.

Chapter 2: Property Rights and Homeowners' Protections

We've established: the notion of squatters' rights frequently suffers misrepresentation--often blown out of proportion by individuals seeking to rationalize their unlawful occupation. They stake claims on properties they have no legitimate right to; however, in reality, the legal system is unequivocal. It staunchly upholds and safeguards lawful property owners' rights against trespassers and squatters.

Merely holding the title as the rightful owner is insufficient; one must proactively establish clear evidence of ownership and take reasonable measures to secure--as well as monitor--their property against unauthorized occupation. Let's explore in-depth: the key property rights homeowners have at their disposal, and all necessary documentation needed for full leverage of those rights.

Fundamental Rights of Property Owners

Laws in the United States and most modern nations around the world recognize property ownership as one of the most fundamental individual rights at their core. Claiming exclusive possession of a residence or parcel of real estate, rightfully acquired by you, not only forms but also bolsters economic freedom and domestic security critically.

You, as the lawful owner of a property, hold paramount rights: these supersede any claims to tenancy or attempted occupation by non-owners. Your core rights encompass -

"The Right of Possession" - You, as the owner, hold exclusive rights to physically control the property and its premises. Legal possession remains unattainable for anyone else without your explicit consent.

2) **The Right to Use and Enjoyment** - The autonomy you possess extends to the utilization of the property, always within adherence to local zoning laws and regulations. You, as an owner, determine whether it serves as your residence or if you rent it out for commercial purposes; furthermore making decisions regarding potential modifications on said property.

3) **The Right of Disposition** - The legal capacity to transfer interest in a property, such as through sale, gift or bequest, is maintained by its owner.

4) **The Right of Exclusion** - The owner, indeed, primarily exercises this right in squatting scenarios: they possess the prerogative to exclude all other parties from the premises; furthermore, it is within their jurisdiction to eliminate any trespassers who unlawfully enter without prior permission.

Property laws and legal precedents at the state and federal levels enshrine these intrinsic ownership rights. Non-owners' attempted occupation or adverse possession claims must yield to an owner's exclusive claim, given they can provide sufficient evidence of their lawful standing.

Across jurisdictions, specific regulations may indeed vary; however, the enduring rights bestowed by legitimate property ownership receive recognition and upholding from an overarching legal philosophy. Without explicit consent from the owner for their presence -- a concession squatters rarely secure -- they have no legal grounds to infringe upon these rights.

Establishing Proof of Ownership

Undoubtedly, mere ownership as the rightful owner isn't sufficient; you must substantiate and validate your claim through verifiable documentation. This evidence plays a vital role in asserting your rights, garnering law enforcement support if necessary - ultimately ensuring success should legal proceedings escalate to that extent.

The official deed records filed with the county or municipality represent the quintessential form of evidence for property ownership. One party transfers their ownership interest and title in a property to another through a legal instrument known as a deed.

Upon purchasing a home, you must ensure that your name(s) feature on the deed; this document is filed in the public record system to establish your legal ownership of the property. It's worth noting, however, there may be additional deeds on file—these could potentially chart chains of ownership transfers throughout the history of said property.

Deed records stand as the most definitive proof of ownership; however, additional supporting documents often exist--these can further fortify your claims:

Title Records: These are the definitive records obtained from a pre-purchase property title search, typically conducted by an attorney or title company to ascertain and confirm the clear ownership of a potential acquisition.

Your mortgage agreement or loan records serve as evidence that you have undertaken the rights and responsibilities of ownership: we refer to these documents as Mortgage/Loan Documents.

You possess an insurable interest as the homeowner: a definitive confirmation is your active insurance policy--the

Homeowner's Insurance Policy--that specifically covers your property.

Your ownership position finds its establishment in the proof you provide: your property tax records--evidence of your payment towards the taxes assessed on a home registered under your name.

Regularly paying utility bills such as electricity, gas, water and others asserts your exclusive ownership of the premises; it reinforces that you indeed use and possess the property.

Compile as much documentation as possible to demonstrate your ownership rights and responsibilities for the property; this will fortify your evidentiary position in case squatters endeavor to cast doubts or levy dubious claims.

Safely store duplicates of all essential ownership documents off-site: this strategy ensures that should your home fall victim to squatters or criminal activity, you can swiftly validate your legal standing with both law enforcement and the judicial system.

Monitoring Ownership Records

The escalating prevalence of property feuds, deed fraud scams and criminal activity in real estate transactions necessitates owners to maintain regular vigilance over county recorder's offices and other public records databases associated with their properties. They should be alert for any suspicious filings that may potentially compromise or obscure their unequivocal ownership title.

Unlawful as it may be, squatters often make audacious attempts to file quitclaim deeds or other dubious property records; their objective is clear: they seek not only to obscure ownership rights – but also prolong legal proceedings against them. Mitigating risks becomes possible when these actions receive early detection and intervention.

Certain counties provide property owner notification services free of charge: these services automatically alert you to any filed or modified documents that may affect your property's records. Alternately, certain third-party monitoring agencies offer fee-based alerts with similar functionality. However—beyond these automated systems—it is crucial for you to conduct regular manual searches and checks; this ensures there are no suspicious activities undermining the integrity of your documentation trail.

Proactively establish, maintain, and safeguard evidence of your legal ownership rights; this strategic approach ensures you can assert your proper standing effectively if squatters ever unlawfully try to possess your property. Do not neglect this critical aspect until an emergency situation arises: take immediate action.

In the upcoming chapters, we will delve into an extensive range of practical prevention methods and security protocols: crucial implementations every homeowner should consider. Our aim is to dissuade squatters from even daring to access or inhabit your premises without permission; therefore, our discourse will pivot around these strategies. You can lay the foundation for decisive action by clearly documenting and defending your ownership rights; it constitutes the legal groundwork.

Part II: Preventing Squatting Incidents

As we solidify our understanding of property rights, legal definitions, and the homeowner's obligations to present clear ownership evidence; we advance towards implementing effective prevention strategies against potential squatters -- a critical task. The adage holds true: An ounce of prevention is indeed worth a pound of cure.

Once squatters gain access to your property and establish continuous occupation for any period, removing them through proper legal channels becomes exponentially more difficult, lengthy, and expensive. The costs can escalate rapidly into the tens of thousands of dollars; furthermore - the emotional toll from such a violation of your home can be utterly devastating.

Hence, every homeowner should prioritize the development of a comprehensive and multi-layered approach to deter squatters from even gaining an initial foothold on their premises. When it concerns safeguarding your single most valuable asset - your home, an active mindset coupled with continuous vigilance is absolutely vital.

In the upcoming four chapters, we shall scrutinize the fundamental pillars of a potent squatting prevention strategy. This plan constructs numerous barriers and safeguards around your property:

Enhanced locks, alarm systems, surveillance and more—these are but a few of the robust physical security measures we implement to control access.

Establishing regular property monitoring protocols, maintaining rigorous inspection routines, and promptly identifying potential intrusion early warning signs; this is the task at hand.

3) The owner must continually maintain clear, well-documented evidence to demonstrate their exercise of possession and use rights over the property.

4) You should actively cultivate a partnership with your local community, neighbors, law enforcement and support services; by doing so--you will ensure that additional vigilant eyes are always watching over your home.

Make your property an undesirable, impractically difficult target for opportunistic squatters seeking easy gains: display visible security measures; establish routine activity patterns that confirm occupancy and integrate community vigilance. This strategy should instantly dissuade aspiring trespassers from attempting unlawful entry.

Homeowners facing elevated risk factors, such as operating vacant properties or maintaining residence away from their homes for extended periods, require an even stronger security protocol. We will outline these enhanced prevention measures to further harden the defenses. Given that each situation is unique: it's advisable to adopt a highly customized approach in preventing potential threats specific to your circumstances.

Naturally, no strategy can promise a flawless 100% prevention of determined criminal squatters' attempts to unlawfully occupy. However - if you implement and uphold comprehensive safeguards - it will place you firmly in control over the situation. In case intrusion efforts emerge, swift detection and cessation before establishing residency become possible; this empowers you to exert your complete legal rights as the proprietor.

Failing to prioritize prevention yields undeniable and significant effects: allowing squatters temporary residence immediately places you in a disadvantaged position. These intruders might manipulate the situation as a precursor for adverse possession claims or present other dubious legal defenses; this is indeed—without question—an imminent risk. The initiation of such risks often commences with simplistic trespassing; however, if left unchecked, it swiftly evolves into an extended conflict over eviction—a situation that is both complex and chaotic.

Every homeowner must avoid experiencing such emotional turmoil and financial nightmare through diligent prevention. Secure your home, the castle you possess, by fortifying its gates and walls against those who might unlawfully seek to invade and occupy it.

Focus and commit to implementing the prevention strategies we will cover in subsequent chapters; by doing so, you establish a formidable deterrent perimeter around your property. Your home should not become an uphill battle for reclamation - this outcome lies well within your control as its owner if you take proactive measures of prevention. When it comes to safeguarding your single most valuable asset, vigilance must prevail: that is the watchword.

Chapter 3: Securing Your Property

When it comes to preventing unauthorized entry and deterring would-be squatters from attempting to take up residence on your property, implementing robust physical security measures is absolutely critical. This foundational layer serves as the first line of defense in your prevention strategy.

At its core, the goal of your security approach should be to control and monitor all access points to the property, creating significant impediments that make unlawful entry as difficult as possible for trespassers. An ideal system leaves no easy openings for squatters to simply walk through.

Let's examine the key elements that should be included in an effective physical security plan tailored to protecting your home from squatters:

Enhanced Lock Systems

Arguably the most fundamental security component, fortifying your locking mechanisms on all exterior entry points is a necessity. This applies to not just your front and back doors, but all windows, garage entries, basement access points, pet doors and any other potential ingress.

At minimum, you'll want to upgrade to high-security lock sets that utilize anti-pick, anti-bump keying technologies and reinforce the strike plate and door frame with extended throw-bolt locking mechanisms. For sliding doors and windows, consider supplementing with anti-lift devices, charley bars, or installing anti-theft window locks.

For vacant properties or if you'll be away for extended periods, explore implementing a full re-keying or electronic lock rekeying program that changes out all locks on a recurring schedule. This ensures previous key holders can't regain entry.

Avoiding easily copied keysets and instead utilizing high-security keys with legal restrictions on duplication can further enhance your lock system's integrity. Technological solutions like smart locks with revised entry codes can allow secure temporary access for service workers without risking key proliferation.

The bottom line is that your lock system should present a formidable first barrier that deters squatters from being able to easily breach entry points through forced tactics. A determined trespasser may eventually circumvent locks if given enough time and tools - but visible high-security fortifications make your property a less appealing softer target.

Alarm System Implementation

A professionally installed and monitored alarm system can act as a potent force multiplier in tandem with robust lock systems. The shrill alerts can frighten off opportunistic trespassers seeking easy entry while simultaneously signaling for police response.

When selecting an alarm provider, opt for services offering 24/7 professional monitoring that will dispatch authorities for all intrusion alerts. Self-monitored or locally audible-only alarms can certainly still provide deterrence, but are more prone to being ignored in some communities.

Implement comprehensive sensor coverage not just on all exterior entry points, but throughout the interior space as well through the use of motion detectors, glassbreak sensors and more. Panic and duress activation buttons placed strategically throughout the home can be lifesavers in high-risk situations.

Beyond intrusion detection components, various enhanced services like two-way voice communication to monitors, video surveillance integration and fire/environmental monitoring modules can add further security value.

If you'll have extended vacancy periods, there are specialized unoccupied property alarm system configurations to consider that can simulate human activity through lighting, audio and camera movement patterns to enhance the appearance of occupancy as an extra deterrent.

Surveillance Cameras and Lighting

Visible security cameras and ample illumination serve as powerful psychological deterrents against trespassing on your property. The prospect of being recorded or monitored creates accountability risks that squatters naturally want to avoid.

Today's digital video surveillance systems can blanket your property's perimeter with high-definition coverage from multiple vantage points. Wireless and wired camera options allow customized placements. Night vision, motion-activation recording and mobile alerts provide 24/7 monitoring capability.

It's advisable to have visible external camera domes to amplify the deterrent effect, backing those up with additional discreet internal cameras to capture any intrusion attempts that may occur. Clear unobstructed line-of-sight views to entry points are ideal.

Complement your camera coverage grid with motion-activated flood lighting to startle squatters and remove any dark shadowed areas they could try to exploit as blind spots. Combining visible illumination with the red glow of camera domes makes your security presence boldly apparent.

Additionally, surveillance signage posted at access points can further strengthen deterrence through legal transparency. Overtly declaring that the premises is monitored can convince squatters your property is too risky of a target to attempt unlawful entry.

Perimeter Hardening and Fencing

For homes on larger lots with more expansive perimeter boundaries to secure, fencing can be an invaluable layer of physical security when properly implemented. Fencing systems don't just deter casual trespassing - they can also force squatters into having to overcome more obstacles to attempt unlawful entry.

Quality materials like ornamental aluminum or steel ensure a robust barrier. Fence toppers like anti-climb spikes, razorwire coils or electric fence security can further enhance perimeter protection. Avoid privacy slats or other easy climbing aids.

Access control points like automated driveway gates with integrated video should control vehicular ingress while still allowing enclosed pedestrian traffic flow. If vacancy periods are expected, consider implementing full perimeter infrared beam detection zones for enhanced monitoring capacity.

For fencing surrounding full property boundaries, avoid any easy external bypass points like unmaintained tree lines or overgrown foliage that could enable fence circumvention. You want a cohesive enclosed perimeter without any gaps or soft spots that could enable squatter entry.

But hardening isn't just about physical barriers - it's also about removing any environmental aids that could assist squatters. Clearing debris piles, boarding up any unsecured structures, trimming thick vegetation and eliminating anything that could help camouflage or enable unlawful occupation on your property.

A well-hardened, monitored perimeter projects an unmistakable display of control and occupancy that can deter all but the most brazen criminal elements. It signals squatters that any attempt at entry will face multiple layers of deterrents necessitating skilled efforts to bypass.

Securing Vacant Properties

Vacant homes, whether between tenants or waiting to be sold, represent prime targets for squatters looking for easy access. Without regular occupancy patterns, these properties can be more vulnerable if not properly secured.

Beyond implementing the core physical security elements like reinforced locks, alarms and surveillance that we've already covered, some additional vacancy-specific measures may be warranted:

- Install permanent steel security panels over window openings

- Use approved anti-entry door barricades and secondary blockades

- Keep the property exterior well-lit, clean and maintained

- Clear any valuables or belongings that could be seen as a burglar attractant

- Post legible No Trespassing/Private Property signage

- Have mail and deliveries securely held rather than accumulating

- Enlist reliable property management, neighbors or security service patrols to monitor regularly

Basically, you want to present an appearance of tight security combined with zero evidence of contents that could suggest vacancy and attract unlawful entry attempts. Removing any squatter's incentives while posing visible deterrents.

For longer vacancy periods, consider having utilities kept active to eliminate red flags around dormant service status. Some property owners even take measures like staged furnishings and vehicle rotation to simulate an occupied look from outside.

Be sure any on-site security services monitor not just the property itself, but also watch for concerning patterns in the surrounding neighborhood. Vacant homes on blocks with rising urban decay, drug activity or homelessness may justify elevated security protocols to counteract elevated risk factors.

While securing vacant properties does involve more preparation work, the last thing you want is to provide an easy opportunity for unlawful occupancy that then leads to a protracted legal battle to remove entrenched squatters. The investment in proper security upfront is well worth mitigating those nightmare scenarios.

Maintaining an Appearance of Occupancy

Our final prevention consideration involves making every effort to continuously project the unmistakable image of active occupancy and vigilance at your property, even during times you may be away for extended periods.

Squatters are inherently looking for easy, unoccupied properties they can slip into with minimal resistance or detection. Homes that clearly demonstrate regular activity patterns, domestic presence and neighborhood awareness become exponentially less appealing targets.

Some proven strategies for reinforcing the appearance of occupancy include:

- Keeping interior and exterior lighting on timers and varied schedules

- Installing smart home systems that can randomize light patterns, music or TV playback

- Leaving a visible vehicle parked in the driveway and rotating vehicle positions periodically

- Having landscaping maintained on a regular schedule with no overgrowth

- Arranging for snow removal, leaf clearing and other seasonal property maintenance

- Utilizing privacy mail stops and hold services so mail isn't accumulating

- Enlisting neighbors or a security service to check on the home regularly

The key concept is to make it undeniably clear to any would-be squatters casing your property that it is actively inhabited and monitored. Avoid any prolonged stretches of inactivity that could signal being an easy score.

For properties you do need to keep vacant for longer terms, having a dedicated property manager make regular walk-throughs is advisable. Their scheduled presence helps deter unwanted activity. You can even have them perform basic tasks like cycling lights on interior/exterior timed schedules.

When combined with robust physical security layers like alarm systems, cameras and perimeter control, the overall portrait projected is one of a defended, occupied home with zero incentive for intrusion attempts versus freely accessible vacancies. That disparity in risk-reward calculus is exactly what will stop the vast majority of opportunistic squatters in their tracks.

Preventing squatters begins with proactively enacting robust physical security barriers that establish unmistakable control and monitoring over your property. Follow through by reinforcing continuous evidence of active occupancy. Create a multi-layered deterrence strategy, and your home simply becomes an impractical, unappealing target not worth an unlawful entrant's invested efforts. That's a winning outcome for any prevention-focused homeowner seeking to protect their most important investment decisively.

Chapter 4: Regular Property Inspections and Monitoring

While implementing robust physical security measures like alarm systems, surveillance cameras, and perimeter hardening is crucial, those protective layers alone are not enough to fully insulate your property against the potential threat of unlawful squatters. Consistent monitoring and inspection routines are equally vital components of any comprehensive prevention strategy.

The reality is that even the most formidable security systems can be circumvented given enough time, resources, and determination by criminal elements. Squatters are often relentlessly persistent, casing properties repeatedly looking for any potential vulnerability to exploit. That's why actively monitoring your home through direct inspections and vigilant observation is so critically important.

By making your presence as the lawful property owner and primary overseer undeniably obvious, you deprive squatters of the opportunity to establish any degree of perceived residency or occupancy claim. Catching unauthorized individuals in the process of attempting entry or conducting pre-operational surveillance allows you to demonstrate your rights while exposing their unlawful intent from the outset.

Let's explore proven monitoring and inspection protocols to incorporate into your prevention practices, ensuring no unlawful occupancy could begin festering undetected on your premises.

Regular Self-Inspection Walk-Throughs

When it comes to hands-on monitoring, nothing beats performing frequent, thorough property inspections in person as the owner or property manager. These physical walkthroughs allow you to examine the entire premises up close, observing any out-of-the-ordinary disturbances that could indicate attempted intrusion or the beginnings of squatter activity.

How often you conduct these self-inspections can vary based on factors like whether the home is occupied full-time, employed as a rental/vacation property, sitting vacant between occupancy, or if you'll be away traveling for extended periods. At minimum, most security experts recommend weekly or bi-weekly walkthroughs as a prudent monitoring cadence.

For vacant properties or homes you'll have limited physical presence at over longer stretches,.augmenting your inspections with supplementary patrols by security services may be advisable to maintain an even higher monitoring frequency.

During your inspection rounds, be vigilant in surveying every area of the property - not just the obvious external entry points. Scour for any signs of forced entry, lock tampering, or fence breaches around the full perimeter. Closely inspect basement and attic access points, detached garages/outbuildings, and any other blind spots or enclosed spaces a squatter could attempt to access discreetly.

Don't just look for obvious indications of break-ins either. Trained inspectors learn to identify more subtle potential warning signs like:

- Discarded food wrappers, beverage containers or other litter

- Makeshift camps or shelters fashioned from tarps/blankets

- Stockpiles of clothing, bags or personal items

- Evidence of human waste or rough bedding areas

- Surveillance blinds/peepholes fashioned from trash bags or materials

- Propped entry points or tampered security devices

Remaining vigilant to detect these kinds of marginal signs can help you catch unlawful residence attempts at the earliest possible stage before they can proliferate into entrenched occupancy situations.

Employing Mobile Monitoring Technology

Of course, diligent property owners can't be physically present on their premises 24/7 to directly monitor for potential intrusion activity. That's where leveraging mobile technology and remote monitoring systems can pay huge dividends in maximizing your vigilance.

Many modern security and home automation platforms incorporate robust mobile apps and web portals that allow remote monitoring of all sensor activity from wherever you may be located. Captured video clips, event alerts, and system arming/disarming can all be managed through these mobile access points.

With smart home integration, you can even remotely view live video feeds, control lighting patterns to promote an appearance of occupancy, or activate audible alarms and deterrence features to disrupt unauthorized individuals on the premises. The ability to virtually monitor in real-time can be a potent force multiplier.

If funds allow, there are also professional remote monitoring services that can provide an extra layer of human oversight beyond self-managed mobile access. With redundant monitoring centers, these services can escalate responses by dispatching police or security personnel to investigate on-site incidents in progress.

While service pricing can vary considerably, some options integrate affordable virtual guard tour capabilities where off-site agents periodically log in to assess video/sensor activity and provide watchful oversight that augments self-monitoring.

Especially during periods of vacancy or extended travel away from the home, taking advantage of these remote monitoring capabilities prevents any gaps in your vigilance that squatters could attempt to exploit undetected. Keeping persistent virtual eyes on your property can go a long way toward snuffing out unlawful activity before it progresses too far.

Property Management & Security Patrol Services

For homeowners who spend significant periods away from their properties due to factors like vacation home ownership, work travel requirements, housing being part of an inherited real estate portfolio, or property maintained in caretaker status pending future decisions - utilizing professional property management or security patrol services can be advisable supplemental monitoring solutions.

Reputable property management firms offer customized services including:

- Scheduled on-site inspections/walk-throughs (interior and exterior)

- Key holding and property access control

- Oversight of maintenance, landscaping, utilities, etc.

- Management of contractors/vendors for upkeep

- Tenant screening, lease execution, rent collection (if applicable)

- Securing premises during vacancy periods

These comprehensive oversight duties provide an invaluable layer of third-party monitoring and care for your asset in your absence. With trained staff regularly attending to the property, the opportunity for undetected squatting attempts becomes extremely narrow. Issues like forced entry, utility irregularities, or other suspicious activity patterns can be swiftly identified and reported for intervention.

For properties facing elevated security risk factors, supplementing with dedicated security patrol services operating on randomized schedules can further harden your monitoring posture. These mobile security officers will routinely tour the premises and surrounding area, providing an active deterrent presence while watching for any concerning activity meriting escalated response.

When combined with centrally monitored alarm systems and mobile virtual monitoring capabilities, layering professional property management and security patrol tours creates an extremely formidable monitoring network that leaves very little maneuvering room for unlawful intruders to operate undetected.

Neighborhood Watch & Community Partnerships

Your monitoring scope extends beyond just your own property lines as well. Fostering strong community connections with neighbors, homeowner associations, and local law enforcement can multiply your detection capabilities against would-be squatters exponentially.

Participating in a formal neighborhood watch program allows you to unite with other proactive residents dedicated to collective security and vigilance across a broader localized area. By working cooperatively through shared communications and watchful presence, the community as a whole can identify and deter criminal activities like squatting before they ever gain traction on individual properties.

Law enforcement authorities also heavily promote neighborhood watch involvement as a proven force multiplier in combating all manner of neighborhood crimes. The more vigilant community members they have empowered as their extended eyes and ears, the more efficient their response capabilities become.

You should build rapport with your community policing division, providing them with key information about your property, occupancy status, security contacts, and any concerns over heightened squatter activity in the area. Supply them with your mobile numbers and monitoring service information so they can rapidly contact you to verify issues or consent for intervention on your premises.

Some law enforcement agencies even support virtual neighborhood watch programs that allow active community members to confidentially log and share reports of suspicious activities digitally. This data is monitored by sworn personnel for identifying crime patterns and deploying appropriate response resources.

The key underlying principle is removing any perception of an "opportunity" neighborhood where squatters could potentially take up residence with minimal risk of detection. By seamlessly integrating monitoring efforts with your localized community and police partners, your prevention net becomes wider and tighter - allowing very little room for unlawful occupation attempts to materialize unnoticed.

Property inspections, remote monitoring capabilities, third-party patrol services, law enforcement cooperation, and community partnerships - bringing all of these reinforcing monitoring elements together creates an imposing multilayered vigilance posture that squatters will be extremely hard-pressed to circumvent undetected.

When the unmistakable reality of your overwatch as the lawful owner is emphatically obvious through every single monitoring channel you've emplaced, opportunistic squatters seeking easy undefended targets will be compelled to look elsewhere. Maintaining that airtight perimeter of unified monitoring leaves absolutely zero openings for unlawful occupation of your home to fester.

Chapter 5: Establishing and Maintaining Evidence of Occupancy

In our discussions so far, we've covered the fundamentals of property ownership rights, the legal framework around squatters' claims, implementing robust physical security measures, and instituting rigorous monitoring protocols. However, one critical element still remains – the importance of continuously establishing and maintaining clear, well-documented evidence affirming your rights as the lawful occupant and resident of the property.

You see, squatters often attempt to make dubious claims that the premises were "abandoned" or exist evidence of active residency by the owner in order to rationalize their unlawful presence. By accumulating an indisputable documentation trail demonstrating your active, ongoing use and control of the property, you inherently undermine any such arguments before they can even be raised.

This chapter focuses on the practices and paperwork trail you should implement to reinforce your status as the rightful legal occupant at all times. Doing so positions you firmly on unassailable legal ground while limiting opportunities for squatters to manufacture narratives about supposed vacancy or neglect.

The Significance of Occupancy Evidence

At its core, the entire concept of squatters attempting to make claims of adverse possession, residency rights, or premises abandonment stems from an inability to demonstrate the owner's active, enduring presence on the property. That ambiguity around occupancy status is precisely the legal maneuvering room squatters try to create.

As the lawful owner and occupant, eliminating any such ambiguity by establishing definitive, sustained proof of your residential control becomes absolutely paramount. You effectively slam the door on squatters' abilities to raise dubious defenses or manufacture adverse possession arguments from the outset.

Furthermore, promptly compiling this evidence stream from day one better positions you to expedite any legal filings or proceedings that may arise due to a squatting incident. The more robust your documentation package validating your occupancy rights, the more efficiently you can proceed in getting law enforcement and the courts to recognize those rights and take action against unlawful intruders.

In short, comprehensively proving your continuous status as the property's legal occupant through verifiable paperwork leaves no gray areas for squatters to exploit. It's a critical prevention tactic to employ alongside the physical security and monitoring measures we've already covered.

Documenting Residency Status

So what specific types of documentation should you accumulate and how do you go about generating this evidence trail? Let's examine some of the key methods for validating your active, entrenched residency at the property:

Utility Bills: Having a continuous stream of utility bills like electricity, gas, water, internet and other services delivered in your name to the property address counts as strong validation of your occupied use of the premises and associated rights.

Be sure to diligently maintain these monthly statements as an ongoing record.

Originating Mail/Deliveries: Similarly, ensuring your regular mail flow is consistently being delivered to the property reinforces your presence as the legal receiver and resident. Having packages or subscription services like newspapers delivered can augment this residency documentation.

Government/Tax Records: Paying property taxes and being listed for municipal services at the home's address in your name serves as official government affirmation of your ownership and occupied status. Retain these records carefully.

Financial Records: Mortgage statements, homeowner's insurance policies, and other financial documentation pertaining to the property help substantiate your vested rights and responsibilities as the live-in owner/occupant.

Personal Records: Dated images and videos taken inside the home capturing your family's presence can provide powerful supplemental proof of residency when embedded with metadata. Leveraging apps and cloud backups to accumulate this visual archive is wise.

Maintenance/Repair Documentation: Retaining invoices, contracts and permits for any work performed on the property helps reinforce the through-line of active maintenance and upkeep you've provided as the responsible owner/occupant.

Lease Documentation (if renting): If the property has tenants residing there, ensuring your copy of the active lease agreement lists you as the owner/landlord can further validate your status.

The key is to create an extensive, continuously updated portfolio containing every type of documentation definitively linking your personal identity to active possession, use and control of the specific property in question over an unbroken period of time. The more overlapping layers of validation contained in this documentation archive, the more overwhelmingly you'll be able to squash any squatter claims of vacancy, abandonment or ambiguous status.

Reporting Suspected Squatters Promptly

Of course, despite your best preventative efforts and exhaustive evidence gathering, there's always a chance that an unlawful attempt to occupy your property could be made by determined criminal squatters. That's why maintaining vigilance through your monitoring protocols is paramount – so you can instantly identify and respond to any suspected squatting activity at the earliest possible stage.

Time is of the absolute essence when it comes to reacting to and reporting suspected squatters on your property. The longer any unlawful occupancy is allowed to proliferate before you intervene, the more complicated the situation can potentially become from a legal standpoint.

Remember, squatters are highly motivated to establish claims of residency and rights, so they'll immediately begin generating their own documentation trail to counter yours if permitted any window of time to entrench themselves. Things like:

- Taking occupancy photos and videos

- Retaining utility activation records in their name

- Backdating leases or fraudulent property records

- Documenting maintenance or changes made to the premises

They're well aware of the legal nuances around occupancy evidence, so they'll aggressively try manufacturing validation aimed at undermining your rights from the outset of any unlawful presence.

That's why initiating the formal process to confront and evict squatters needs to begin with your swift reporting as soon as they're detected on the property. Immediately file detailed reports with law enforcement documenting the incident and providing your evidence file affirming your rights as owner/occupant. This properly establishes the legal record right away.

When squatters are confronted and ordered off the premises from that position of authority on day one, you inherently deny them any ability to fabricate counter-narratives about their supposed residency claims. Your evidence stream is already firmly cemented. They have no legal footing to stand on thanks to your proactive measures.

Some homeowners make the mistake of temporarily overlooking suspected squatter activity, assuming they can simply handle the situation on their own terms down the road. However, that elapsed time can frequently lead to preventable complexities and strengthen the squatters' position through continued occupation.

By maintaining vigilant monitoring and instantly reporting unauthorized occupants while presenting your overwhelming residency documentation up front, you eliminate so many of the potential pitfalls that can make squatting cases drag into protracted legal battles. Those first crucial days of action are vital for asserting your rights conclusively.

By establishing and diligently maintaining your evidence portfolio validating continuous occupancy as the property's rightful owner, you effectively close the door on squatters' abilities to generate meritless claims against your rights from the moment they attempt unlawful entry. Your documentation becomes an invaluable asset for expediting the process of enforcing your legal protections swiftly and decisively. Leave no stones unturned - overwhelmingly prove your status and commitments as the lawful resident.

Part III: Dealing with Squatters

As dedicated as we've been in exploring comprehensive prevention strategies so far, the unfortunate reality is that even the most proactive and security-conscious homeowners may still find themselves in the nightmare scenario of having to confront squatters who have unlawfully occupied their property.

Despite implementing robust physical deterrents like alarm systems and surveillance, maintaining vigilant monitoring routines, and establishing exhaustive documentation validating your occupancy rights - the simple fact remains that criminal elements are relentlessly determined to find ways to circumvent preventative measures in pursuit of their own self-interests.

This harsh truth underscores why prevention alone is never enough when it comes to safeguarding your home against squatters. Having a proven action plan for decisively dealing with unlawful occupants and restoring your property rights is an absolute necessity as well.

If you do find yourself facing an active squatting incident already in progress, do not allow panic or despair to set in. Maintaining a rational mindset and avoiding any reckless actions that could jeopardize your legal standing is crucial in this high-stress situation. Rest assured that as the lawful property owner, you still maintain the upper hand from a rights perspective - provided you follow the appropriate procedures for having squatters formally removed.

Over the next three chapters, we'll methodically explore the precise protocols and legal processes you need to follow in order to efficiently and safely resolve squatting situations and restore the sanctity of your home:

First and foremost, we'll outline the proper methods for initiating the formal eviction process while adhering to all due process requirements. The specific notification procedures, filing steps, and documentation obligations will be covered. Understanding the role of law enforcement and the judicial system will also be explained.

From there, we'll provide guidance on gathering all necessary evidence and building an ironclad legal case to present during eviction proceedings. The types of proof to compile, witnesses to document, procedures for serving notices, and requirements for each phase of the eviction lifecycle will be described.

Finally, we'll empower you with strategies for effectively navigating the complex legal system, covering topics like hiring and working with attorneys, potential defenses and arguments squatters may attempt to raise, as well as insight into the mindsets and tactics often employed by persistent professional squatters.

At its core, this section is about restoring your proper authority as the lawful owner and reestablishing control over your property through authorized legal channels - not reckless self-help measures that could ultimately undermine your position further. We'll remain grounded in advocating ethical, rightful, and legal means for resolving squatting situations in a manner that vindicates your full ownership rights.

Unfortunately no prevention plan can achieve 100% effectiveness, which is why having resolute determination and the right removal game plan is so vital. Your most valuable financial asset and the very sanctity of your home demands nothing less than absolute commitment to doing whatever is necessary to purge unlawful occupants through the appropriate judicial processes.

So take reassurance in the reality that as the legal owner and occupant, the law ultimately remains on your side against squatters - provided you follow sanctioned procedures diligently. Our mission over the coming chapters is ensuring you understand those processes in full, empowering you to resolutely stand your ground and reclaim what is rightfully yours without flinching or ceding any ground to those attempting to infringe upon your property rights.

Your home is your sanctuary, your legacy, your life investment. Do not allow squatters to rob you of those sacred privileges without an uncompromising fight to evict them through every entitled legal avenue. We'll show you how to navigate those avenues with confidence and rightful force.

Chapter 6: Understanding the Eviction Process

As much as we'd prefer to never have to put these protocols into practice, the reality is that many homeowners will at some point face the daunting challenge of legally removing entrenched squatters from their property. Despite your most diligent prevention efforts, the resourceful determination of criminal opportunists can occasionally penetrate even the most formidable security measures.

When that nightmare scenario arises, understanding and adhering to the appropriate legal processes for eviction becomes absolutely vital. Deviating from sanctioned procedures by taking ill-advised "self-help" actions could not only drastically undermine your position, but potentially expose you to criminal or civil liabilities. Squatters are well-versed in attempting to manipulate nuanced legal principles for their own gain.

That's why comprehensively mastering the formal eviction process flow within your local jurisdiction needs to be a top priority. Having a clear roadmap for asserting your lawful property rights through the appropriate judicial mechanisms can be the difference between swiftly resolving the incident and becoming mired in a protracted legal quagmire.

Let's dive into the crucial eviction protocols every owner should understand and adhere to when forced to remove squatters from their premises.

Understanding the Role of Law Enforcement

Perhaps one of the most frequent misconceptions homeowners have is assuming that law enforcement can simply arrive on the scene and immediately remove squatters upon request once their trespass is reported. Unfortunately, it's not quite that straightforward in the majority of jurisdictions.

In most locales, the process of evicting squatters from an occupied property is treated as a civil legal matter between the disputing parties, rather than a criminal trespassing issue for police to intervene directly. Law enforcement's role is to keep the peace and refer the parties to follow the proper eviction filing procedures through local housing courts.

While it may seem counterintuitive that criminal trespassers refusing to vacate aren't removed by police, the complex legal principles around evaluating claims of property rights, potential adverse possession arguments, and jurisdictional nuances typically necessitate formal eviction lawsuits without oversight rather than summary police action.

That being said, law enforcement absolutely still plays a vital role for property owners - just one that requires filing formal eviction process paperwork first in order to trigger their direct enforcement capabilities. Some of the key ways police can assist once the process is initiated include:

- Keeping the peace and deterring potential violence or breaches between owners and squatters.

- Issuing official trespass warnings and notifications as a first step in some jurisdictions.

- Physically removing squatters from the premises once a court order is issued.

- Investigating and forwarding for prosecution any criminal acts committed by squatters after trespass.

From the outset of a suspected squatting incident, it's prudent to file an official report with your local police documenting the unlawful occupation and affirming your property ownership evidence. This properly establishes the record while demonstrating your respect for following sanctioned legal channels.

Police reports also help justify calls for emergency presence and documentation of any criminal behavior like destruction of property, theft, threats, or refusal to comply with posted orders during the eviction proceedings.

Understanding law enforcement's supportive role within the defined due process parameters for eviction is critical for owners. While they can't unilaterally extract squatters, their assistance throughout the formal procedures is invaluable for restoring your property rights safely and defending against any escalations by hostile occupants.

Initiating the Formal Eviction Process

Once law enforcement has been properly noticed of the squatting issue, initiating the formal eviction lawsuit process is the next crucial step for property owners. While specifics vary by location, the general flow involves:

Service of Notice to Quit: As the first formal action, a written "Notice to Quit" document must be drafted and properly served to the unknown occupants/squatters on the premises according to statutory specifications. This establishes the official eviction notice timeline, typically ranging from 3-30 days.

Filing the Eviction Lawsuit: If the squatters fail to voluntarily vacate by the notice deadline, official eviction documents must then be filed with the appropriate local housing court or judicial authority overseeing the process. Required documentation includes ownership verification, copies of prior notices served, and sworn statements affirming the presence of squatters.

Service and Court Appearances: After case filing, the squatters must then be officially served with a court summons and complaint documentation. Multiple scheduled court dates are set, requiring both property owners and squatters to appear and state their cases before a judge if the squatters refuse to leave.

Obtaining the Court Order: Provided the weight of evidence sides with the lawful property owner after court arguments, the judge will ultimately issue an official Writ of Restitution or court order legally instructing the squatters to vacate by a specified deadline date. This order then enables law enforcement to forcibly remove noncompliant occupants if still remaining.

Reinstating Lawful Possession: Once the ordered move-out date passes with the premises still illegally occupied, law enforcement can formally enforce the court's ruling by arriving to physically remove the squatters and restore the owner's legal repossession and control of the property.

Throughout this entire sequence, it's absolutely vital that property owners follow these formal court procedures to the letter with no deviations or self-help actions taken outside the legal process. Vigilante attempts at "do-it-yourself" evictions like changing locks, removing belongings, shutting off utilities or using force/intimidation against squatters could completely derail the case.

Not only does this open owners up to potential civil liabilities, but it effectively nullifies the position as an innocent lawful party following due process. Judges tend to view such actions very dimly and could rule against owners essentially condoning the squatter occupation they initiated illegally.

Navigating the Court Eviction Process

Given how pivotal the housing court litigation phases are within the overall eviction process, it's worth providing some additional insights around what to expect and some of the common roadblocks owners may face:

Documentation is King: Thoroughly documenting and evidencing your legal ownership rights with deeds, mortgage paperwork, tax records and more is vital. Squatters will attempt to sow ambiguity about your claims.

Serving Occupants Properly: Precise compliance with all notification mandates about service, timeline durations and appearance dates is critical. Defects can delay cases extensively.

Identifying All Occupants: Owners are required to identify all unknown individuals on the premises in filings. Partial identifications can hinder complete evictions.

Cash for Keys Considerations: If squatters appear legitimate but down on their luck, owners may offer a "cash for keys" payment to vacate quickly without contesting.

Obeying the Court Order: After obtaining the final judgment, squatters cannot legally be removed until the specified deadline passes and law enforcement is present.

Documenting Damages: Any property damages, thefts, or other criminal behavior should be extensively cataloged with evidence for potential prosecution or restitution claims.

Steadfast Determination: Be prepared for squatters to leverage every delay tactic available in hopes you'll eventually get frustrated and give up. Perseverance is necessary.

This process is not a quick resolution by any means due to all the required due process steps. However, provided homeowners maintain diligence, document properly, and allow the system to play out - the court ruling will ultimately reinforce their lawful ownership rights and evict the squatters.

It's a test of fortitude dealing with the bureaucracy and potential games squatters may try to play. But so long as you hold firm to following sanctioned protocols while compiling evidence methodically, courts will rectify the situation in your favor as the rightful owner.

The eviction process may seem arduous, but it represents the principled path for homeowners to reclaim their property through established legal channels while upholding vital housing rights. Armed with patience and adherence to due process requirements, the system can restore your lawful control and deliver justice - one that extrajudicial self-help actions would only undermine.

Chapter 7: Gathering Evidence and Building a Case

As we explored in the previous chapter, successfully navigating the formal legal process to evict squatters from your property hinges upon your ability to develop a comprehensive and persuasive evidentiary case that affirms your rights as the lawful owner. Any potential gaps or discrepancies in documenting the situation can provide openings for squatters to insert dilatory tactics or spurious defenses.

Ensuring you have an airtight body of proof validating both your ownership standing as well as the existence of unauthorized occupants on the premises is absolutely vital. This documented record becomes the crux of your eviction filings with the courts and carries immense weight through each subsequent phase of litigation.

In essence, you must treat the entire process of evidence gathering and case assembly with a mindset akin to building a vigorous legal prosecution against the squatters. Leave no stone unturned in amassing the documentation trail that will withstand scrutiny and decisively swing judicial rulings back in your favor as the rightful homeowner and victim.

Let's delve into the specific evidence types to focus on, the record-keeping best practices to employ, and insights for partnering most effectively with law enforcement and judicial authorities throughout this crucial aspect of confronting squatters.

Documenting Unlawful Occupancy

From the moment you first suspect or confirm unauthorized individuals have taken up residence on your property, assiduous documentation of their unlawful presence must begin immediately. Time is of the essence, as squatters will simultaneously initiate their own efforts toward establishing occupancy rights narratives the longer they remain.

Some of the key evidence you'll want to start compiling includes:

Photographic/Video Documentation: Capture detailed still images and video footage providing clear visual evidence of the squatters and their occupancy encampment on the property from various vantage points. Prioritize entry areas and rooms where belongings have been moved in. Leverage smartphone metadata to embed GPS coordinates and timestamps validating when and where images were recorded.

Property Inspection Reports: Whether conducting the inspections yourself or utilizing a property management service, generate detailed written reports documenting observations of squatter activity and occupation during each visit. Narrate all access breaches, damage assessments, confiscated belongings, encountered individuals and their statements, etc. Have these reports officially signed, dated and notarized.

Eyewitness Accounts/Statements: If neighbors, delivery workers, utility employees or any third parties have directly witnessed squatters accessing or occupying the premises, obtain official written statements from them recounting what they observed. These sworn eyewitness testimonies lend crucial third-party confirmation to your account of events.

Subject Identification Documentation: Make a concerted effort to gather personal identifying details about the squatters themselves to the greatest extent possible. Full legal names, dates of birth, physical descriptions, employment details, vehicle information, social media profiles and any other available intelligence can prove invaluable - especially if criminal prosecution ultimately becomes an option down the line.

Entry Evidence Collection: When it is safe to do so, carefully document and collect any physical evidence of forced entry or staged entry techniques utilized by the squatters. Photograph and catalog things like damaged locks, makeshift laddering and climbing materials left behind, jimmy tools, security camera footage of break-in attempts and more.

The overarching principle is to create an exhaustively detailed documentation stream that establishes a coherent, verifiable timeline of the squatting violation transpiring without any lapses or ambiguity that occupants could attempt to distort. The more thoroughly you capture visuals, written reports and third-party eyewitness validation, the more formidable your body of evidence becomes.

From day one, an evidence-first methodology puts you firmly in control of the truth narrative surrounding your case. Instill that diligence from the initial stages, leaving zero openings for occupants to obfuscate later as litigation proceedings ramp up.

Maintaining the Documentation Trail

Of course, merely accumulating stacks of paperwork and digital files will not suffice for presenting an effective case through the formal legal channels. You must be exceedingly diligent in organizing, updating and preserving the evidence archive in a cohesive, reviewable manner.

Haphazardly throwing documentation into boxes or computer folders is a recipe for confusion and mismanagement that squatters will gladly exploit to poke holes in your case. Maintaining a pristine record-keeping protocol is vital.

This discipline begins with rigorous data capture practices at every stage of your evidence accumulation. Whenever documenting squatter occupancy visually or through written reports:

- Record precise dates, times and locations using metadata wherever possible

- Catalog items systematically and consistently using a standardized naming/numbering system

- Backup data regularly to secure cloud storage locations with version tracking

- Hash and encrypt sensitive evidence files containing personal details

- Redact copies for privacy and safety prioritization as needed

For general documentation guidelines to adhere to:

- Use a dedicated evidence binder or folder system organized chronologically

- Index and paginate accumulated paperwork in the correct sequence

- Maintain a detailed evidence log spreadsheet tracking each item gathered

- Cross-reference specific items to relevant events and timelines

- Utilize readable tabbing or categorization systems for easy reference

- Retain original copies of critical items like leases, deeds, contracts, etc.

- Back up redundant copies of the complete evidence archive off-site

This level of neurotic record-keeping may seem excessive, but attention to evidentiary detail is what will win legal battles against squatters determined to obfuscate facts.

The more organized, comprehensive and structured your documentation packages are from the very beginning, the easier it becomes to efficiently build persuasive case filings and exhibits for each juncture of the eviction process. Scrambling to put together a cohesive record at the last minute is a preventable pitfall too many owners stumble into.

Collaborating with Law Enforcement

While you as the property owner are ultimately driving the evidence gathering and case development process, it's critical to recognize the indispensable partnership role law enforcement can and should play throughout these efforts. Attempting to go it completely alone risks missed opportunities for expanding your documentation resources.

From your very first inkling of suspected squatter occupation, initiating dialogue and information sharing channels with the relevant police authorities needs to be a top priority. Some key collaboration priorities include:

Providing Complete Ownership Documentation: Share copies of your deeds, titles and a comprehensive ownership packet validating standing as soon as making the initial report. Police need this evidence to initiate their involvement.

Sharing Squatter Intelligence: Any identifying details, background information, belongings and personal effects related to the specific individuals squatting can greatly aid police in developing investigative leads.

Supplying Event Reports and Chronologies: Furnish copies of your accumulated inspection reports, witness statements and other evidence materials so officers have full case context moving forward.

Authorizing Police Property Access: Provide keys or security codes permitting officers to access the premises for evidence collection and occupant encounters as needed.

Requesting Official Notifications: If your local jurisdiction has specific squatter notification protocols officers initiate, advocate for those procedures to commence and generate more documentation.

Reporting New Violations and Damages: Immediately report any escalated violations, threats, criminal mischief or safety issues created by squatters so police can respond accordingly.

From their side, police should reciprocate by sharing copies of official reports generated, documentation of actions taken, statements obtained from squatters and results of any investigations conducted on an ongoing basis.

Establishing this symbiotic, cooperative relationship with law enforcement creates a feedback loop that strengthens both parties' evidence arsenals simultaneously. They provide professional verification of events through reports you can incorporate into your filings. You supply first-hand context that enhances their enforcement response.

It's a team effort between victim and police, centered on mutual evidence amplification and case fortification aimed at ensuring the strongest possible judicial outcome for the lawful property owner.

Leveraging Law Enforcement Partnerships

Beyond just streamlining evidence sharing and coordination with officers assigned to your specific case, it's also worth forging broader operational partnerships with law enforcement entities that can enhance your prevention and response capabilities.

Some key areas to explore collaborative avenues include:

Rapid Response Prioritization Programs: Many police agencies offer specialized hotlines or prioritized dispatch capabilities for reporting in-progress squatting situations at enrolled properties. This can accelerate evidence gathering and prevention of new damages.

Homeless Outreach and Diversion Services: Departments often have dedicated resources for conducting humane outreach with non-violent squatters, offering temporary shelters or services to discourage continuance of illegal occupation.

Mobile Field Evidence Collection Support: Certain jurisdictions can deploy special field evidence technicians trained in advanced forensics and data collection methods for strengthening criminal cases against problematic occupants.

Joint Investigative Initiatives: If your area is experiencing high volumes of organized squatting activities, cooperating as a complainant witness for longer-term investigations targeting ringleaders can unlock additional enforcement resources.

Community Outreach Programs: Local law enforcement just about universally appreciates responsible community partners willing to host public education initiatives focused on legal occupancy rights, squatters awareness and being a good neighborhood witness.

The possibilities for leveraging law enforcement assets in creative, mutually-beneficial ways beyond the routine case reporting protocols are extensive. Which specific programs or capabilities are available to you will require proactive inquiries with the appropriate special units, community relations divisions and investigative task forces in your jurisdiction.

It's worth investing time into developing these external partnerships, especially for property owners dealing with chronic squatter issues or concentrated activity across multiple holdings in high-risk areas. Expanding your cooperative networks amplifies your access to professional evidence gathering and enforcement resources exponentially.

And again, the core principle remains maintaining comprehensive documentation through assiduous record keeping and continual evidence sharing with these law enforcement partners. The deeper truth and fact-finding efforts go, the more insurmountable your case becomes against squatters deploying misinformation.

Truthfully, no homeowner relying solely on their own isolated evidence gathering efforts can ultimately amass as formidable a final case package as those collaborating symbiotically with law enforcement's broader resources and legal authority. Unlocking that strategic force multiplication through professional partnerships is a case-winning advantage responsible owners should prioritize.

So begin establishing those liaison channels immediately, maintaining an ethic of complete transparency and constant communication with assigned units throughout your documentation journey. With the combined weight of your diligence and law enforcement's validation, any squatter's ability to manufacture false narratives collapses under the overwhelming assembled truth.

Chapter 8: Navigating the Legal System and Seeking Representation

As we've established over the previous two chapters, effectively navigating the formal eviction process and compiling a formidable body of evidence to affirm your rights as the lawful property owner are both absolutely vital when forced to confront squatters. However, those two elements alone still do not guarantee securing a favorable outcome through the complex legal system squatting cases require.

The truth is, while you may feel confident in your ability to represent yourself during eviction proceedings armed with robust documentation - underestimating the nuanced challenges you'll likely face in housing court against savvy squatters could prove a costly miscalculation. These unlawful occupants are frequently quite versed in attempting to exploit legal loopholes and technicalities to their advantage.

Combine that with the often maddening inefficiencies inherent to an overworked judicial system processing hundreds of eviction filings, and the situation soon becomes a recipe for frustration and potential missteps by well-intentioned yet ill-equipped property owners representing themselves pro se (without an attorney).

That's why heavily considering enlisting professional legal representation should be a top priority once squatters take up occupation of your premises. While hiring a qualified attorney certainly constitutes an additional expense amid the financial damages you're already suffering as a victim, the strategic value of having a housing law expert advocate in your corner throughout these proceedings cannot be overstated.

Let's examine the compelling reasons to secure representation, along with insights for vetting and working effectively with legal counsel. We'll also explore some of the common legal defensives squatters may attempt so you can counter them with the appropriate strategies under your attorney's guidance.

The Value of Professional Legal Counsel

Perhaps the most obvious benefit of hiring a dedicated attorney to handle your squatting case is their mastery and experience in navigating the extremely nuanced arena of landlord-tenant laws, property rights legislation, and the complex rules of civil procedure governing housing court venues.

While you may have diligently researched and studied up on eviction protocols, attorneys who specialize in this judicial realm operate with far more in-depth and up-to-the-minute expertise honed over years of immersive practice. They know all the substantive and procedural nuances inside and out cold, coached by years of firsthand experience.

Especially when dealing with seasoned professional squatters adept at attempting to manipulate counterintuitive legal theories and hyper-technical arguments about rights far beyond what a self-represented homeowner may anticipate - having a zealous advocate laser-focused on dismantling those tactics becomes absolutely invaluable.

Skilled attorneys leverage extensive repositories of case law, judicial precedents, local protocols and established arguments refined from volumes of relevant experience the average homeowner simply cannot access or match on their own. That privileged knowledge represents an unfair disadvantage if you lack professional representation yourself when squaring off against savvy, sovereignty-aligned occupants.

Beyond mere subject matter expertise, accomplished housing counsel also offer invaluable strategic guidance throughout the judicial process. They can provide advice on:

- Optimal timing and procedures for filings

- Dealing with improper service, evidence challenges and other common landmines

- Interacting with clerks, judges, marshals and other legal stakeholders

- Leveraging subpoena powers and investigative authorities for fact-finding

- Negotiation tactics for potential cash for keys or alternative dispute resolutions

- Lines of legal argumentation and affirmative defenses to deploy

- Procedural loopholes to carefully avoid sabotaging your position

- When to initiate contempt proceedings, appeals and criminal referrals

- Orchestrating post-eviction restoration of possession and damage mitigation

Additionally, maintaining attorney-client privileged communication insulates your discussions of legal strategies and evidence from any opposing efforts at forced disclosure or cross-examination that pro se litigants would lack.

While there's certainly no substitute for your own diligent efforts in documenting evidence and compiling the fact pattern, attorneys ensure that diligent work translates optimally into persuasive argumentation and seamless procedural compliance through their professional expertise.

So while self-representation may seem like a tempting cost-saving route - the truth is that fumbling through the legal minefield alone risks far more catastrophic financial outcomes, not to mention the incredible stress and frustrations that can compound throughout a protracted proceeding. For most property owners facing the already traumatic scenario of squatters violating their home, securing professional legal advocacy provides priceless peace of mind.

Selecting and Working With an Attorney

Of course, not all legal representation is created equal - so being judicious in vetting and selecting an attorney tailored to your specific needs is crucial. A poorly chosen or incompatible counsel can doom cases quicker than going it alone in some instances.

When evaluating potential attorneys or law firms, be sure to closely examine factors like:

Relevant Practice Area Experience: Prioritize prospects with robust, specialized experience handling landlord/tenant disputes, eviction proceedings, and ideally direct familiarity with squatters' cases.

Proven Track Record With Case Results: Request case lists of representative prior outcomes they've secured for similar property owner victims. Dig into details and ask about any losses.

Local Jurisdictional Knowledge: Housing laws can vary significantly across municipalities, so prioritize attorneys well-versed in your area's precise nuances and stakeholders.

Trial and Litigation Capabilities: While most cases settle, you want counsel prepared and able to follow through with extensive litigation if opponents drag proceedings out unreasonably.

Fee Structure Transparency and Terms: Hourly, contingent, and retainer billing options exist - so clarify your financial commitments and fee scales upfront while avoiding any conflicts of interest.

Client Service and Communication Standards: Maintaining transparency and consistent update pipelines on case progress represent core client expectations to establish early.

Personal Rapport and Compatibility: You'll be communicating extensively throughout this process, so ensure personalities and working styles align from the start.

You may opt to seek referrals from trusted colleagues, property management services, or even law enforcement liaisons. But ultimately you'll want to conduct formal consultations and firm vetting yourself as the working relationship established can make or break your case experience.

Once an attorney is retained, providing them with unrestricted access to your compiled documentation package and aligning on an evidence-driven approach toward case construction should commence immediately. Be responsive to any requests for supplemental materials or testimony preparation, while also maintaining open communication channels to remain apprised of strategy developments and preliminary opposition tactics.

Most crucially, defer to your attorney's advice and guidance once representation initiates. Outside attempts to personally respond to suspect claims, file motions, or represent your case's position can quickly undermine the integrity and admissions at issue. Fully channeling your role as client and assistive evidence provider while empowering your counsel's lead role as legal strategist yields optimal results.

Maintaining this cohesive symbiosis between an organized, forthcoming client and a taking-charge, expert-driven attorney provides a formidable deterrence against even the most well-versed professional squatters and their theorized legal arguments. When the weight of truth, procedural rigor, and strategic advocacy all coalesce decisively on your side, defeating meritless squatter defenses becomes far more tenable.

Countering Common Squatter Claims and Strategies

Of course, even in partnering with highly skilled legal representation, it's still important for property owners to approach this process armed with some general awareness of the types of legal theories and obfuscation tactics squatters frequently attempt in order to undermine legitimate eviction proceedings.

While the specific claims and defenses may vary based on jurisdiction and the unique fact patterns involved, some of the more prevalent strategies your attorney should be prepared to counter include:

Adverse Possession/Residency Rights Claims: You can expect manufactured arguments about having established residency through continuous possession for prerequisite durational periods, hence acquiring tenant rights subject to formal eviction protocols rather than mere trespass.

Evidence Sufficiency Challenges: Despite overwhelming documentation, squatters often try muddying waters around ownership standing, identity verification of occupants, timeline accuracies and more.

Bankruptcy Filing Delays: Familiarity with how certain bankruptcy petitions can trigger automatic eviction stay periods and bought time for unlawful occupants is essential.

Countersuit and Lawsuit Threats: Frivolous countersuits related to fair housing violations, discrimination claims and other bad faith intimidation tactics should be anticipated.

Jurisdictional Disruption: Cases can face abrupt venue changes, removals to federal court, and other delays through dubious jurisdiction challenges over minor irregularities.

Service and Notice Disputes: Squatters consistently raise hyper-technical challenges centered on improper service, notice defects and filing irregularities.

Possession and Standing Arguments: Squatters often dispute basic evidentiary presumptions like what constitutes possession, right of entry conditions and verification burdens.

Your attorney should work proactively to insulate your position against as many of these potential squatter maneuvers as possible through rigorous case construction and affirmative litigation strategy deployed early and aggressively.

Rather than ceding ground by responding defensively to squatters' specious claims, truly accomplished counsel understands the need to seize and maintain firm control of the evidentiary record, while dictating legal momentum through streamlined court procedure mastery.

Anticipating the rhetoric and tactics sure to be levied against you allows your team to preemptively develop and execute persuasive counterarguments, supported by indisputable evidence repositories while leveraging your standing as the unambiguous property owner-victim.

When opposition rhetoric inevitably strays into distortions surrounding key issues like lawful standing, continuous possession, and jurisdictional authorities - your counsel can forcefully redirect proceedings back to the fundamental premises and bedrock principles surrounding homeowner property rights. Judges tasked with efficient docket management appreciate focused, evidence-driven cases avoiding manufactured sideshows.

Coupled with tactical expertise around leveraging favorable judicial rules, compelling motions practice, and aggressive settlement posturing where advantageous, a team well-prepared to dismantle squatter narrative fallacies ultimately prevails.

Because at the end of the day, the law remains unambiguously aligned on the side of lawful property owners against trespassing occupants - provided your arguments adhere to substance over distraction, and your evidence leaves no doubts around ownership validity. Professional counsel guides you toward those just resolutions.

So make no mistake, securing competent legal advocacy is not about ensuring some last-minute "hired gun" patching operation to salvage a poorly constructed case. Rather, it represents a proactive, pivotal investment in zealous rights protection from Day 1 - allowing for strategic, evidence-driven offense from a posture of judicial strength.

Armed with truth and bolstered by an accomplished housing litigation practitioner, the squatter's gambit of exploiting nuances while fabricating delay tactics becomes an exercise in futility. The merits align decidedly in your favor as lawful owner, reinforced by proper case construction and steadfast procedure adherence under your attorney's guidance.

Your violations counsel squarely when egregious opportunists defy property entitlements. But with professional advocacy at the fore, delivering the accountability and justice you're righteously owed becomes far more achievable through our nation's impartial judicial system.

Part IV: Prevention and Policy Recommendations

The preceding sections of this book concentrate on comprehending squatters' rights, securing your property, and navigating the legal system; nonetheless, recognizing that safeguarding your home necessitates a more extensive approach beyond individual efforts is crucial. To formulate effective prevention strategies and policy recommendations demands collective action coupled with community involvement. In this segment: we will delve into fostering an alert neighborhood—elucidating awareness—and advocating for policy alterations to enhance homeowners' rights protection.

The strength of a united community stands as one of the most potent tools in preventing squatting incidents. Neighborhood watch programs, by fostering collective responsibility and vigilance, serve to deter potential squatters effectively and swiftly identify suspicious activities. Such instrumental roles emerge from these programs encouraging residents' mutual surveillance for each other's safety; urging them to report any uncommon events - all while maintaining close collaboration with local law enforcement authorities.

Indeed, we must prioritize raising awareness about squatting issues: numerous homeowners might remain oblivious to potential risks and legal complexities. By implementing public education campaigns; organizing community forums - forging partnerships with local organizations in the process - we can equip individuals with not just knowledge but also resources vital for robust property protection.

Furthermore, we must acknowledge: the fight against squatting transcends personal and communal endeavors. Local, state, and national levels necessitate policy recommendations; advocacy efforts at these tiers can profoundly contribute to addressing this issue. Through a meticulous analysis of current laws and regulations--we identify opportunities for enhancement; subsequently proposing amendments that more effectively protect homeowners' rights.

Potential policy recommendations: impose tougher penalties for squatting offenses; streamline the eviction process--this could deter potential squatters. Additionally, enforce stricter requirements to establish adverse possession claims as a measure of prevention. Further advocacy is essential–it should focus on augmenting funding and resources allocated to law enforcement agencies so they can prioritize promptly responding to squatting incidents; this will bolster overall effectiveness in prevention efforts.

Policy changes often necessitate persistent advocacy and lobbying efforts: this is a crucial point to underscore. Through collaboration with advocacy groups, legal organizations--and elected officials in particular—we can not only elevate awareness of the challenges confronting homeowners but also champion legislative action that places property rights at the forefront.

Ultimately, homeowners must adopt a multifaceted approach: it combines individual vigilance; community engagement--and most importantly—policy reform. By nurturing this culture of collective responsibility and pushing for stronger protections, we will significantly advance our efforts to safeguard properties; at the same time, preserve the sanctity of our homes.

Chapter 9: Community Involvement and Neighborhood Watch Programs

The strength of a united community proves invaluable in the battle against squatting. Although securing and protecting your property through individual efforts is crucial, significantly enhancing our ability to prevent and address squatting incidents relies on fostering collective responsibility and vigilance. This chapter explores the importance of community involvement, delving into neighborhood watch programs' significance; it also investigates strategies for raising awareness—promoting both vigilance—and forging partnerships with local authorities.

The Power of Community

Not only is squatting a concern for individual homeowners, but it also poses risks to the safety, security, and overall welfare of an entire community. By uniting as one force, we stand strong against those who aim to unlawfully inhabit and trespass on our properties. A tight-knit community has the power to dissuade potential squatters by communicating unequivocally that such behavior will not be accepted; moreover, a vigilant network stands prepared for immediate response.

A well-informed and proactive community can function as an early warning system: it rapidly detects any suspicious activities or signs of unauthorized occupation, nipping squatting incidents in the bud. This collective vigilance prevents these issues from escalating into complex legal battles.

Neighborhood Watch Programs: A Proactive Approach

The establishment of neighborhood watch programs represents an exceptionally potent method for leveraging community power. Such initiatives unite residents under a common objective: to maintain safety and security within their locality. Through the cultivation of transparent communication, elevation in awareness levels, and stimulation of vigorous engagement; these programs assemble a vigilant network capable not only identifying squatting threats but also responding to them swiftly.

Key elements of successful neighborhood watch programs include:

1. **Holding regular meetings and communicating consistently:** This enables residents to disseminate crucial information and engage in debates over concerns, fostering a collaborative environment for strategizing against issues like squatting that plague the neighborhood.

2. **Organized neighborhood patrols:** Conducted by skilled volunteers, these patrols can monitor and report any suspicious activities or signs of unlawful occupation, aiding in maintaining community security.

3. **Partnerships with Law Enforcement:** It is crucial to build robust alliances with local law enforcement agencies; through regular communication and collaboration, a rapid response to squatting incidents can be guaranteed, information sharing can occur

expeditiously, and resources will become more accessible.

4. **Education and Awareness Campaigns:** These ongoing campaigns maintain a well-informed community about squatting risks, its legal implications, and necessary property protection measures; they play an integral role in disseminating this crucial knowledge.

5. **Monitoring Vacant Properties:** A system that actively monitors and reports vacant or unoccupied properties can deter them from becoming targets for squatters.

Neighborhood watch programs, by instilling community pride and ownership, empower residents to actively safeguard their homes and neighborhoods.

Raising Awareness and Promoting Vigilance

Raising awareness about the issue of squatting and promoting vigilance among residents initiates effective community involvement. Some strategies that can be employed include:

- **Hosting community forums and workshops:** this action can serve as a platform for educating residents on squatters' rights, legal implications, and prevention strategies. More precisely--when we invite not only legal experts but also law enforcement officials; when homeowners who have experienced incidents of squatting join us--valuable insights surface along with first-hand accounts.

- **Developing and disseminating informative materials such as brochures, flyers, and social media campaigns:** these actively contribute to the spread of awareness--equipping residents with vital knowledge: they can identify potential squatting situations and promptly report them.

- **Neighborhood Signage:** By strategically positioning signage in high-risk areas or vacant properties, the community signals its vigilance and intolerance for unlawful occupation to potential squatters; thus serving as a powerful deterrent.

- **"Neighborhood Networking":** We advocate for the establishment of neighborhood groups, online forums, or messaging channels; such initiatives not only facilitate information sharing but also cultivate a strong sense of community solidarity against squatting.

- **Establishing Clear and Accessible Reporting Mechanisms:** We can enhance residents' prompt reporting of potential squatting incidents or suspicious activities by setting up clear, accessible mechanisms - for instance, dedicated hotlines or online portals.

We can empower our communities to recognize the signs of squatting and take proactive measures--through heightened awareness and promoted vigilance. This way, they will be able to protect their properties and neighborhoods.

Partnerships with Local Law Enforcement and Authorities

Paramount to our mission is not only community involvement, but also the forging of robust partnerships with local law enforcement agencies and authorities. These alliances can guarantee a coordinated--and potent--response to squatting incidents; furthermore, they offer indispensable resources for neighborhood watch programs: an integral part in maintaining safety within communities.

- **Regular Communication and Collaboration:** By regularly establishing channels of communication with local law enforcement agencies, we can facilitate the exchange of crucial information. This includes updates on potential squatting situations as well as devising coordinated strategies to address incidents.

- **Training and Education:** Law enforcement officials may equip neighborhood watch volunteers with the necessary knowledge and skills—essential for accurate identification of squatting incidents, as well as their proper reporting in compliance with legal protocols.

- **Developing clear protocols and channels for rapid response:** These measures can ensure prompt notification to law enforcement agencies, enabling swift intervention in confirmed squatting incidents.

- **Resources and Information Sharing:** When partnering with local authorities, one gains access to valuable resources--legal expertise, property databases; and information-sharing mechanisms become available. These tools are instrumental in not only preventing squatting cases but also resolving them swiftly.

- **Collaborating with local authorities on Community Outreach Programs:** can foster awareness, educate residents, and encourage a proactive approach towards addressing squatting issues and other concerns related to neighborhood safety.

Communities can enhance their efforts in preventing and effectively addressing squatting incidents by forging robust partnerships with local law enforcement and authorities; such alliances allow them to leverage not only their resources but also legal authority--a crucial tool for tackling these issues.

Conclusively: community involvement and neighborhood watch programs wield significant power in combating squatting. The collective strength of a united community, when harnessed—through awareness-raising efforts; promotion of vigilance within its ranks—and forging alliances with local authorities can create an imposing deterrent against unlawful property occupation. Together we possess the capability to safeguard not only our homes but also our neighborhoods - thereby preserving a paramount sense of security.

Chapter 10: Policy Recommendations and Advocacy

Individual efforts and community involvement prove crucial in safeguarding our properties against squatters; yet, we must recognize that the battle against unlawful occupation transcends mere spatial boundaries. To effect lasting change--to forge a more secure environment for homeowners--advocacy and policy reform often become imperative at local, state, and national levels.

This chapter delves into: potential policy recommendations; amendments to current laws and regulations--particularly exploring measures that local authorities and communities can implement. The emphasis, throughout this discussion, remains on the critical importance of advocacy efforts – specifically lobbying–in protecting homeowners' rights.

Analyzing Existing Laws and Regulations

To propose policy changes, one must first critically analyze the current legal framework that encompasses squatting, trespassing and property rights. Although laws differ among jurisdictions; frequently there exist opportunities for enhancement or clarification to enhance homeowner protection and discourage potential squatters.

The complexity and length of the eviction process for removing squatters from a property emerge as a common concern. Frequently, legal procedures become convoluted, time-consuming, and costly for homeowners; this could potentially extend the emotional and financial toll inflicted by squatting situations. By streamlining these processes - yet not compromising on due process or fairness – we may alleviate some burden on property owners.

The legal definition of squatting and the differentiation between squatters and trespassers merit thorough examination. In certain jurisdictions, these distinctions can blur; this ambiguity may result in confusion or even provide exploitable loopholes for individuals aiming to illegally inhabit a property. By establishing clear, unambiguous definitions -- and pairing them with fitting penalties for offenses -- we can communicate a more potent deterrent message while also enhancing legal safeguards for homeowners: an essential step towards maintaining homeowner security in our society.

Moreover, a critical imperative exists to scrutinize the laws and regulations that govern adverse possession claims. These provisions can occasionally empower squatters, granting them ownership rights over a property following sustained occupation for specific time duration. Although historical roots and justifications underpin the concept of adverse possession, potentiality may exist in enhancing requirements and safeguards as preventive measures against abuse while preserving legitimate property owners' rights.

Potential Policy Recommendations

An analysis of current laws and regulations yields several potential policy recommendations; these suggestions could significantly enhance our strategy to tackle squatting issues while safeguarding homeowners' rights.

- Advocating for reforms that streamline and expedite the legal processes of evicting squatters--all while ensuring due process; this approach not only could alleviate homeowners' burdens but also dissuade potential squatters from unlawful property occupation.

- Advocating for the fortification of laws concerning trespassing and squatting, we aim to establish a more robust deterrent: imposing stiffer penalties and consequences for these offenses. Through this action-- sending an unequivocal message that such actions will not be tolerated--we strive towards greater societal order.

- Clarifying Definitions and Requirements: As we strive for clearer, more unambiguous legal definitions of squatting, trespassing, and adverse possession; furthermore -- by establishing stringent requirements for claiming adverse possession-- we can potentially close loopholes. This action would ultimately enhance homeowner protections.

- Enhancing Property Owner Protections: We advocate for property owners, striving to secure additional legal safeguards and protections: expedited court proceedings; more accessible legal representation - all while dedicating resources specifically towards addressing squatting incidents. Our aim? To equalize the playing field–empowering homeowners in their battle against unlawful occupation.

- Increased Funding and Resources: To enhance the effectiveness of prevention and enforcement efforts, we must push for increased funding and resources within law enforcement agencies; this prioritization will enable prompt responses to squatting incidents at a local level.

- Public Awareness and Education Campaigns: Proposing comprehensive public awareness and education campaigns on squatting, property rights, and legal remedies can equip communities with the necessary knowledge to safeguard their homes; it also empowers individuals to take proactive measures.

The Role of Local Authorities and Communities

Engaging proactively with local authorities and communities to address the issue of squatting is equally as important as formulating policy recommendations and advocating at state and national levels.

Local governments and municipalities can pivotally implement measures and initiatives to discourage squatting, while supporting homeowners' rights. Potential proposed actions may include:

- Advocating for the establishment of dedicated squatting task forces or specialized units within local law enforcement agencies serves a crucial purpose: it prioritizes and promptly responds to squatting incidents. This approach not only enhances response times, but also provides focused expertise in handling these cases at hand.

- Vacant Property Registration and Monitoring Programs; implementation of these programs receives encouragement: this could aid in identifying--and subsequently securing--unoccupied properties, thereby diminishing their vulnerability to potential squatters.

- Community Outreach and Education Initiatives: By collaborating with local authorities on the development and implementation of community outreach and education initiatives, we can not only increase awareness about squatting but also foster vigilance among residents. Furthermore, this strategic partnership will empower residents with essential knowledge– equipping them to safeguard their properties effectively–thus promoting a stronger sense of security within our locality.

- Support for the Neighborhood Watch Program: We seek collaboration and support from local authorities to establish and empower neighborhood watch programs, thereby enhancing community efforts in identifying--and promptly reporting--potential squatting situations.

- Legal Aid and Assistance Programs: Advocating the creation or expansion of legal aid and assistance programs - specifically tailored to help homeowners navigate squatting cases, thus protecting their rights - could furnish them with critical support; furthermore, it would equip them with indispensable resources.

Fostering partnerships between local authorities and community organizations--such as neighborhood associations, homeowners' associations, or advocacy groups: this strategic alliance could pave the way for a coordinated, collaborative approach. An approach capable of addressing squatting issues; furthermore promoting homeowners' rights emerges as an effective solution through such cooperative efforts.

The Importance of Advocacy and Lobbying

Securing the implementation of measures that protect homeowners' rights and effecting meaningful policy changes often necessitate sustained advocacy and lobbying efforts. The challenging, time-consuming process, however, remains a necessary step towards creating an environment wherein property owners feel safer and more secure.

Various forms can embody advocacy efforts: they range from grassroots campaigns and petitions; extend to organized lobbying, even engaging with elected officials--those policymakers we hold in high regard. Advocates have the power to influence the legislative process by raising awareness, educating stakeholders – presenting well-researched compelling arguments: this enables them not only a voice but also an ability–a potent force indeed–to push for policies that prioritize homeowners' rights while addressing squatting issues effectively.

Like-minded organizations, legal experts, and community groups: by forging coalitions and partnerships with these entities--we can amplify the impact of our advocacy efforts; simultaneously lending credibility to our cause. Furthermore - if we leverage media power along with social platforms – they serve not only as tools for raising public awareness but also as mechanisms to garner support while applying pressure on decision-makers towards action.

Recognizing the essentiality of persistent, patient, and unwavering commitment is a key factor in successful advocacy and lobbying efforts. These are not one-time endeavors; rather they form an ongoing process. Engaging with policymakers sustainably, continuously monitoring legislative developments, and adapting strategies as circumstances evolve all stand crucial to achieving success in advocacy campaigns.

Ultimately, we can forge a more secure and equitable legal environment--one that not only safeguards our properties but also upholds the sanctity of our homes: this is achievable through combining grassroots efforts; strategic lobbying, and an unwavering commitment to homeowner rights.

Conclusively: Individual and community efforts remain paramount in addressing squatting incidents -- yet, to effect lasting change; a comprehensive approach is necessary. This involves policy reform, collaboration with local authorities– particularly through sustained advocacy and lobbying efforts. Through critical analysis of existing laws and regulations; proposing policy recommendations; as well as engaging in targeted advocacy campaigns--we can actively work towards creating a safer, more secure environment for homeowners. This strategy also serves to deter potential squatters while upholding the fundamental rights of property ownership.

Conclusion

As we conclude our journey through the pages of this book, it's essential to reflect on the invaluable insights and strategies we've explored for protecting our properties from squatter threats. Our traversal has been comprehensive, navigating legal intricacies, exploring practical prevention measures, and harnessing collective power through community engagement.

In our exploration, we plumbed the intricacies of squatters' rights and their governing legal frameworks. We discovered that adverse possession and squatters' rights, despite originating from historical roots, can serve as tools for those aiming to unlawfully occupy properties. Balancing protection for legitimate claims with prevention of abuse is a nuanced endeavor that necessitates an in-depth understanding of laws and regulations differing across jurisdictions.

Emphasizing proactive measures, we underscored their importance in property security and deterring potential squatting. Our strategies range from implementing robust physical safeguards to maintaining an appearance of occupancy. Regular inspections also contribute significantly, serving as a critical element toward creating formidable barriers against unlawful occupation.

We acknowledge the potency of documentation and record-keeping. By establishing and maintaining clear evidence of occupancy, such as utility bills and mail, along with meticulous record-keeping, we can dissuade squatters and fortify our legal position, crucial should the need to navigate the eviction process or defend our rights in court ever arise.

Confronted with the regrettable truth of squatting incidents, we delved into the nuanced legal eviction procedures, underscoring the importance of following due process and eschewing vigilantism. Gathering evidence emerged as a pivotal step, fortifying our cases and facilitating effective collaboration with law enforcement and legal authorities for successful resolutions.

Our journey transcended the limits of mere individual efforts; we understood the deep influence that community engagement and neighborhood watch programs can exert in deterring and addressing squatting incidents. Cultivating a collective ethos marked by responsibility and vigilance empowers us against such threats, enabling us to defend our rightful ownership.

Further, we delved into policy recommendations and advocacy, recognizing that concerted efforts at various levels often require lasting change. Our exploration included potential amendments to existing laws, measures for locally-based authorities, and underlined the importance of sustained homeowner rights protection through ongoing lobbying and advocacy efforts.

Reflecting on the book's presented wealth of knowledge and strategies, a central theme emerges: proactive vigilance in safeguarding properties is essential. Merely acknowledging risks and strategies falls short; we must actively implement necessary measures to fortify our homes and communities.

We, as homeowners, must actively embrace the responsibility of guarding our properties. Through fostering open communication, sharing information, and collaborating actively with neighbors, local authorities, and advocacy groups, we can create a formidable force against those seeking unlawful property occupation.

Advocacy and lobbying efforts pivotally drive this pursuit, swaying the legislative landscape to prioritize homeowners' rights and create a more secure and equitable environment for property owners.

Our journey towards safeguarding properties is not a sprint but a marathon, requiring perseverance, vigilance, and an unwavering commitment to home sanctity protection. Armed with knowledge, community engagement, and determination, we can chart a path to a future where squatting incidents are distant memories. Let's embrace action, take up responsibility, and passionately advocate for change, ensuring home sanctity persists across generations.

About the Author

Alheri Farouq, a dedicated lawyer, specializes in property law and real estate litigation. Her keen interest lies not only in protecting homeowners' rights but also promoting community safety; thus she directs her legal practice towards providing practical solutions for issues related to property ownership and occupancy.

Farouq, who holds a prestigious law degree, has actively navigated the complex legalities of property disputes and fought for fair and transparent judicial processes. Her specialization in landlord-tenant relationships coupled with her deep understanding of housing rights empowers her to assist clients effectively: she equips them with necessary knowledge to safeguard their homes against an array challenges – squatting incidents being one such issue.

"Home Protectors: A Guide to Safeguarding Your Property Against Squatters" represents Farouq's authorship, wherein she imparts her insights and expertise; this empowers readers with actionable strategies for protecting their properties. Leveraging from her legal background--coupled with an unwavering commitment towards community advocacy-- Farouq dispenses practical advice; she guides homeowners through the intricate pathways of property ownership, enabling them to defend their rights effectively.

Farouq, through her work, aspires to contribute: she aims towards the creation of safer--and more secure-- communities. She envisions homeowners feeling confident; their properties protected and the sanctity of homeownership preserved.

www.ingramcontent.com/pod-product-compliance
Lightning Source LLC
Chambersburg PA
CBHW050041260726
48658CB00005B/1718